SWEET CAROLINA

copyright © 2022 by *Our State* magazine.
All rights reserved.
Published by *Our State* magazine, Mann Media, Inc.
PO Box 4552, Greensboro, NC 27404
(800) 948-1409 | ourstate.com
Printed in the United States by LSC Communications

No part of this book may be used or reproduced
in any manner without written permission.

EDITOR IN CHIEF: Elizabeth Hudson
SWEET CAROLINA LEAD EDITOR: Katie Schanze
EDITORS: Todd Dulaney, Katie Kane, Mark Kemp,
Katie King, Chloe Klingstedt, Katie Saintsing
DESIGN DIRECTOR: Claudia Royston
ART DIRECTOR: Jason Chenier
EDITORIAL DESIGNERS: Erin LaBree, Hannah Wright
PHOTOGRAPHY COORDINATOR: Renee Saunders
Library of Congress Control Number: 2022908287

ON THE COVER:
Fresh berries, fluffy cake, and sweet whipped cream
come together in our cool and creamy strawberry
icebox cake. Find the recipe on page 72.

COVER: MATT HULSMAN; BACK COVER: TIM ROBISON

SWEET CAROLINA

CLASSIC SOUTHERN PIES · CHARMING BAKERIES · OLD-FASHIONED CANDY

In the Old North State, saving room for dessert is a piece of cake.

In North Carolina, late spring heralds strawberry season. Sun-sweetened, sugar-glazed berries like these make a pie to remember.

SWEET PLACES

Western

- 6 The Hop Ice Cream Café, Jack the Dipper, French Broad Chocolate Lounge
- 7 Miss Angel's Heavenly Pies
- 8 Dolly's Dairy Bar & Gift Shop
- 9 Justus Orchard
- 10 McFarlan Bakery
- 12 Dillsboro Chocolate Factory, The Pie Safe Baking Company, The High Test Deli & Sweet Shop
- 14 Asheville Bee Charmer

Piedmont

- 16 Krispy Kreme
- 18 Maxie B's
- 20 Videri Chocolate Factory
- 21 Black Mountain Chocolate Bar
- 22 Escazú Chocolates
- 24 The Humble Bee Shoppe
- 25 Dewey's Bakery, Winkler Bakery
- 26 Sweets by Shayda, Strong Arm Baking
- 27 Black Magnolia Southern Patisserie
- 28 Cake & All Things Yummy
- 29 Sherry's Bakery
- 30 Hayes Barton Café and Dessertery
- 31 Rockford General Store
- 32 Maple View Ice Cream
- 33 Burney's Sweets & More
- 34 The Candy Factory

Eastern

- 36 Mickey's Pastry Shop
- 38 The Peppered Cupcake
- 39 Sunset Slush
- 40 Britts Donut Shop
- 41 Celtic Creamery
- 42 Calabash Creamery
- 43 Surfin' Spoon, Rachel K's Bakery, The Fudgeboat
- 44 Cakes by Becky
- 45 Orange Blossom Bakery & Café

Jams & Jellies

- 46 Garnet Gals, Mrs. Ruth's Jams, Wildflour Bakery, Imladris Farm, Blue Ridge Jams

SWEET STORIES

- 50 Atlantic Beach Pie
- 52 Snow Cream
- 56 Moravian Cookies
- 58 Sweet Tea
- 60 Diner Pie
- 64 Banana Pudding
- 66 Ice Cream

SWEET RECIPES

- 70 Fried Apple Pies
- 72 Strawberry Icebox Cake
- 74 Strawberry Sonker with Dip
- 76 Dark Chocolate Mocha Cherry Cookies
- 77 Chocolate Chess Pie
- 78 Chocolate Cream Cheese Pound Cake
- 80 Black Walnut Hummingbird Cake
- 82 Coconut Cream Pie
- 84 Buttermilk Pound Cake with Vanilla Cream Cheese Frosting
- 85 Pineapple Pig Pickin' Cake
- 86 Cheerwine Poke Cake with Cream Cheese Glaze
- 88 Honeydew Sorbet Float
- 89 Banana Pudding
- 90 Blackberry Cobbler
- 92 Atlantic Beach Pie
- 93 Molasses Cream Pie Cookies
- 94 Pecan Bourbon Pie

Cake & All Things Yummy

SWEET PLACES

At shops across the state, sweet slices, creamy scoops, and decadent chocolates prove that you *can* buy happiness.

At Celtic Creamery, everything is made from scratch: including the hot, fresh mini doughnuts, which serve as the base for sundaes like the "Surfer's Special." To learn more, see page 41.

SWEET PLACES WESTERN

THE HOP ICE CREAM CAFÉ
Asheville

The Hop has been an Asheville icon since 1978. Current owners Greg and Ashley Garrison continue the tradition with five locations and flavors as artistic and creative as the city itself. Try blueberry kale or a vegan flavor, like strawberry pepita milk.

640 Merrimon Avenue No. 103
(828) 254-2224
thehopicecreamcafe.com

JACK THE DIPPER
Sylva

At the "Home of the Warm Waffle Cone," the aroma of vanilla, chocolate, and cinnamon cones greets you at the door.

280 Asheville Highway, Suite 4
(828) 586-9441
jackthedipper.com

FRENCH BROAD CHOCOLATE LOUNGE
Asheville

Pick up handcrafted bonbons in unique flavors that celebrate Asheville and its surrounding farmers and producers — like strawberry balsamic and sorghum caramel.

10 South Pack Square
(828) 252-4181
frenchbroadchocolates.com

Miss Angel's Heavenly Pies
Mount Airy

Angela Shur's path to becoming a professional baker didn't begin in the kitchen. It started when her husband, Randy, a semiretired farmer, planted 100 fruit trees on the slopes of their Surry County farm. Rather than try to sell baskets of apples, they combined her love of baking with an overabundance of fruit, turning a weekend hobby into a storefront on North Main Street in Mount Airy within a year. Today, the aroma of fresh dough and baked fruit lures passersby into her shop, Miss Angel's Heavenly Pies.
— *Mickie Bare*

153 North Main Street
(336) 786-1537, missangelsheavenlypiesinc.com

SWEET PLACES   WESTERN

Dolly's Dairy Bar & Gift Shop
Pisgah Forest

Located within steps of Pisgah National Forest and within a few miles of dozens of storied sleepaway camps in the Brevard area, Dolly's sits at the crossroads of many summertime comings and goings in the mountains. The shop is a well-known local landmark for hikers, campers, and cyclists headed into or out of Pisgah, and for many families as they launch and close camp week. A field trip to Dolly's has been a special and spirited outing for generations of campers, who clamber aboard buses and bellow out songs the whole way there and back. Many beloved flavors are named for those summer camps (like Camp Highlander, aka coffee cookie fudge), providing another chance to proclaim our loyalties to our camp and affection for our favorite cone. — *Sheri Castle*

128 Pisgah Highway
(828) 862-6610

JUSTUS ORCHARD
Hendersonville

At this pick-your-own apple orchard, it's hard not to be enchanted by the crisp air, the rolling mountains, and the sweet, irresistible scent of cider doughnuts and fried apple pies. The cinnamon-coated doughnuts, a longtime tradition at Justus, roll off the conveyor belt in front of customers; the hand pies are one part Mutsu apple and one part nostalgia, and these days, it's hard to find them anywhere else.

187 Garren Road
(828) 974-1232, justusorchard.com

At Justus Orchard, in addition to the famous doughnuts and fried hand pies, you'll find apple fritters, caramel apples, and whole apple pies.

SWEET PLACES   WESTERN

McFarlan Bakery
Hendersonville

McFarlan has been a mainstay since 1930. Co-owner Michael Cole's father bought the business from Earl McFarlan in 1952 — the same year that Michael was born. Michael grew up working in the bakery, eventually learning to make cookies and pies from real bakers — "the old-timers that really knew how to bake," he says.

Most of the recipes and the methods of making them have never changed. In fact, only Michael and one other person know the secret formula for the famous gingerbread men. "Some things," he says, "you just can't improve on." — *Katie King*

309 North Main Street
(828) 693-4256, mcfarlanbakery.com

PHOTOGRAPH BY TIM ROBISON

Festive gingerbread reindeer and classic gingerbread men are staples at **McFarlan Bakery** thanks to a recipe that dates to 1930.

11

SWEET PLACES WESTERN

DILLSBORO CHOCOLATE FACTORY
Dillsboro

Using single-origin Venezuelan cacao instead of a blend of beans, this chocolatier crafts high-quality truffles (above), chocolate-covered espresso beans, almond bark, and more.

28 Church Street
(828) 631-0156, dillsborochocolate.com

THE PIE SAFE BAKING COMPANY
Forest City

Pie Safe — located in a century-old former bank building that inspired its name — offers apple, pecan, and chocolate chess pies, plus much more.

102 West Main Street
(828) 263-6212, piesafebakingco.com

THE HIGH TEST DELI & SWEET SHOP
Bryson City

Locals still call this popular deli The Filling Station, its original name. For a special treat, order the ice cream sandwiches on homemade cookies (opposite), with creative flavor combinations like green apple ice cream between salted caramel cookies.

145 Everett Street
(828) 488-1919, thefillingstationdeli.com

PHOTOGRAPHY BY TIM ROBISON

12

SWEET PLACES WESTERN

Asheville Bee Charmer works with beekeepers across Western North Carolina and the world to source raw honey.

Asheville Bee Charmer
Asheville

Take one step inside Asheville Bee Charmer in the heart of downtown and you're in honey heaven. The store is stocked with bee-themed everything, from T-shirts and hats to honey-infused soaps and skincare. But what stands out the most are the shelves piled high with jars of gleaming, golden honey. Welcome to the hive. Hope you brought your sweet tooth: The shop urges visitors to not only browse dozens of honey variations — tupelo, orange blossom, wild flower, clover — from across the region and the world, but also to sample them at the honey bar with the help of a personal *bee*-rista.
— *Katie Quine*

38 Battery Park
(828) 505-7736, ashevillebeecharmer.com

SWEET PLACES | PIEDMONT

Krispy Kreme's glowing sign is a siren call, a thoroughly North Carolinian expression of "carpe diem."

Krispy Kreme
Winston-Salem

The story of doughnuts in North Carolina begins in 1937, when Vernon Rudolph opened up shop in Winston-Salem with a recipe purchased from a New Orleans chef. The rest came later: the paper hats, the "Hot Now" light, the iconic white-and-green box. You can imagine the thrill Rudolph must have felt when he took that first bite. You've felt it, too, many times over: the thin layer of sweet glaze giving way to the warm interior, just chewy enough to sink your teeth into. The sensation is unmistakable. And although it's available around the globe now, we know there's a taste of North Carolina in every bite. — *Katie Saintsing*

krispykreme.com

SWEET PLACES PIEDMONT

Although Maxie B's coconut custard pie — a North Carolina tradition — is too fragile to ship, the bakery can send pecan and chocolate chess pies right to your doorstep.

Maxie B's
Greensboro

Customers from around Guilford County and beyond have long flocked to Maxie B's for its decadent cakes. In 2017, owner Robin Davis expanded the menu to include pie. As with cake, Davis was motivated by her own cravings for "authentic, Southern, classic recipes." Maxie B's customers love pie as much as she does, Davis says, and each recipe has developed a devoted following.

— *Claire Cusick*

2403 Battleground Avenue, Suite 7
(336) 288-9811, maxieb.com

SWEET PLACES PIEDMONT

VIDERI CHOCOLATE FACTORY
Raleigh

You'll feel like a real-life Charlie at this bean-to-bar chocolate factory. The golden ticket: chocolate bars that range from classic milk and dark chocolate to flavors like blueberry and pink peppercorn.

327 West Davie Street
(919) 755-5053
viderichocolatefactory.com

Explore Videri Chocolate Factory on a self-guided tour before eating dessert. The hardest part is making a decision.

PHOTOGRAPHY BY BRYAN REGAN, DHANRAJ EMANUEL

BLACK MOUNTAIN CHOCOLATE BAR
Winston-Salem

Cocoa beans from the Dominican Republic become peppermint bark, espresso brownies, layer cakes, and salted caramel tarts at this artisan chocolate factory and, yes, *actual* bar — a rotating menu of sweet craft cocktails means you can drink your dessert.

450 North Patterson Avenue, Suite 110
(336) 293-4698, blackmountainchocolate.com

SWEET PLACES | PIEDMONT

Whether you call them truffles or bonbons, Escazú's confections — in flavors like peanut butter caramel and Earl Grey ganache — are almost too pretty eat. *Almost.*

Escazú Chocolates
Raleigh

Forget a nightcap — cozy up with a cup of drinking chocolate in flavors ranging from chocolate chai to peanut butter to white chocolate and spices, or try one of Escazú's "historic hot chocolates," based on recipes from as far back as the 1500s. For an edible souvenir, fill a box with jewel-colored, "paint"-splattered, gold-dusted confections so beautiful they could pass as works of art. Inspired by a trip that cofounders Danielle Centeno and Hallot Parson took to a cacao farm in Costa Rica, Escazú was the first bean-to-bar chocolate shop in Raleigh when it opened in 2008 — and one of just a few in the entire country. More than a decade later, they still source their beans directly from small farms in Costa Rica and Venezuela, roast and grind them using antique equipment, and then handcraft them into small-batch chocolate bars, truffles, ice cream, drinking chocolate, and more. — *Katie Schanze*

936 North Blount Street
(919) 832-3433, escazuchocolates.com

SWEET PLACES PIEDMONT

THE HUMBLE BEE SHOPPE
Winston-Salem

True to her name, owner Brittany "Bee" McGee has always loved bees and celebrates them at her bakery. Custom confections include a rainbow's worth of macarons, stunning buttercream cakes, and treats like oatmeal raisin cookies made only from plants. Honeybees — the original vegans — would approve.

1003 Brookstown Avenue
(336) 293-7457, thehumblebeeshoppe.co

DEWEY'S BAKERY
Winston-Salem

For nearly a century, Dewey's has been honoring the homemade baking tradition with its famously thin Moravian cookies. Today, traditional spiced ginger and sugar cookie thins are joined by Meyer lemon, brownie crisp, salted caramel, and toasted coconut flavors, and sold nationwide.

**262 South Stratford Road
(336) 725-8321, deweys.com**

WINKLER BAKERY
Winston-Salem

Many of the methods at this Moravian bakery haven't strayed much from those used when it was established in 1807. Today, Winkler is a beloved tourist stop in Old Salem, where, on Saturdays, costumed docents use old-fashioned tools to roll out and bake Moravian cookies. But there's also another traditional sweet that endures at Winkler: sugar cake, a yeast-raised coffee cake that's coated in layers of melted butter before being topped with a blanket of brown sugar and cinnamon.

**521 South Main Street
(336) 721-7302, oldsalem.org/winkler**

Winkler's Moravian sugar cakes are baked in an oven that is still heated with wood as it was nearly 200 years ago.

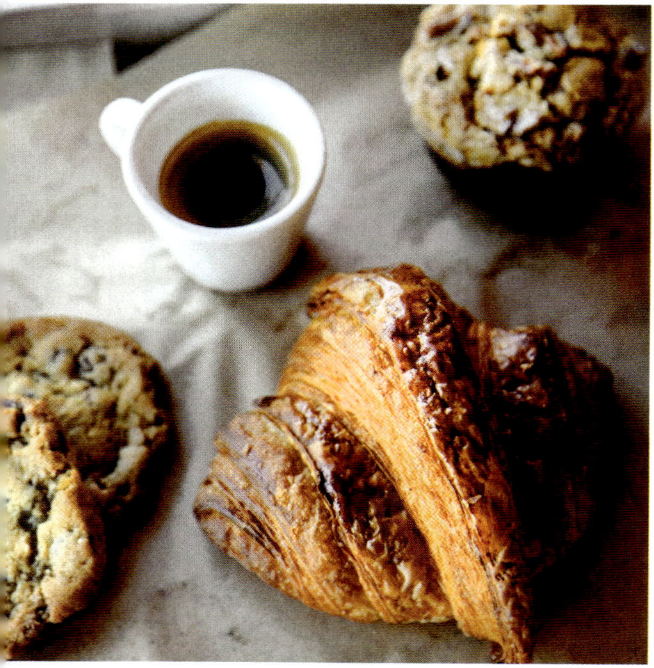

STRONG ARM BAKING

Oxford

Julia and Thomas Blaine have been making doughnuts, cookies, croissants (left) brownies, breads, and other baked goods using ingredients sourced from local farms since 2014. The couple, regular vendors at several farmers markets, recently opened their first brick-and-mortar location downtown.

117 Main Street
(919) 339-4350
strongarmbaking.com

SWEETS BY SHAYDA

Durham

Shayda Wilson, a Cordon Bleu-trained pastry chef, opened this shop to capture the spirit of a French bakery and found sweet success. The rainbow-colored macarons (right) taste as good as they look.

105 West Morgan Street, Suite 105
(919) 454-4015
sweetsbyshayda.com

THIS PAGE: ANNA ROUTH BARZIN, ERIC WATERS; OPPOSITE: DHANRAJ EMANUEL

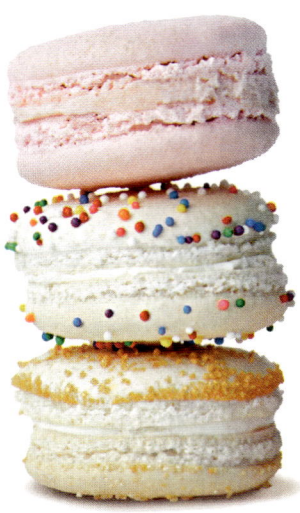

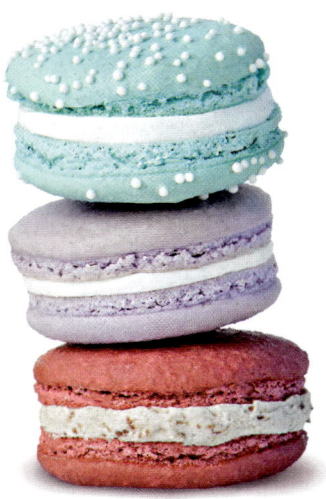

Black Magnolia Southern Patisserie

Greensboro

You might *think* you've had a great cinnamon roll, but have you ever had a $5,000 cinnamon roll? The judges of General Mills' 2020 Neighborhood to Nation Recipe Contest knew they had when they sampled Greensboro baker Veneé Pawlowski's bourbon "banoffee" pecan cinnamon roll with banana-cinnamon filling, bourbon-banana caramel, English toffee, and toasted pecans. The cash prize helped Pawlowski expand her side business into a bakery known for French classics with indulgent Southern flavor combinations.
— *Robin Sutton Anders*

For more information, call (336) 355-0592 or visit blackmagnoliagso.com.

SWEET PLACES | PIEDMONT

CAKE & ALL THINGS YUMMY
Kernersville

Jumbo cupcakes in fun flavors like orange Creamsicle, pineapple upside down cake, and vanilla bean latte are owner Sabrina Dixon's specialty, but visitors also find intricately-decorated sugar cookies, chocolate-covered marshmallows (below), and more.

103 East Mountain Street
(336) 310-4504, cakeandallthingsyummy.com

Sherry's Bakery
Dunn

Southern-style, multilayer cakes with zebra-like icing stripes elicit gasps when they're cut into. But for those of us who have neither the talent, the tools, nor the steady hands required to use them, thank heavens for our local cake ladies.

In Dunn, everyone knows they can count on Sherry Baysa, whose 10-layer yellow cake with chocolate frosting is available every day beginning at 6 a.m. One dig through layer upon layer of dark brown and sunshine yellow will convince you why, until 1967 — when Baysa's parents renamed it after their young daughter — the bakery was called Dunn Rite. — *Susan Stafford Kelly*

122 North Wilson Avenue
(910) 892-3310
facebook.com/sherrysbakerydunn

Eight, 10, 12 layers — or more! Sky-high cakes are a point of pride in the South.

SWEET PLACES PIEDMONT

Hayes Barton Café and Dessertery

Raleigh

Since 1998, owners Marget and Frank Ballard have served up homestyle favorites, but it's Marget's giant cakes that have brought the café the most recognition. Most days, a line forms outside the restaurant as people swing by to purchase a slice of chocolate cake topped with Kahlúa-soaked Heath Bar; lemon-blueberry with vanilla bean cream cheese frosting; or peanut butter, chocolate, and banana "King" cake. Perhaps the biggest compliment comes from the Ballards' youngest customers — it's not uncommon for kids to press their noses against the dessert display case and lick the glass. — *Chloe Klingstedt*

2000 Fairview Road
(919) 856-8551
hayesbartoncafeanddessertery.com

One of Hayes Barton's best sellers is the classic coconut layer cake.

ROCKFORD GENERAL STORE
Dobson

At Rockford, big glass jars are filled with old-fashioned candy, but customers come for servings of peach, sweet potato, cherry, and berry sonker — the sorta-pie, sorta-cobbler dessert found only in Surry County — to eat right at the oilcloth-covered table or take home for later. The 200-year-old Scotch-Irish tradition — no one knows the origin of the name "sonker" — calls for a plain pie crust on the sides and top of a bowl, fruit mixed with sugar, a bit of butter, and 40 minutes in the oven. Warm fruit juice soaks the crust, and cold ice cream makes it perfect.

5174 Rockford Road
(336) 374-5317, rockfordgeneralstore.com

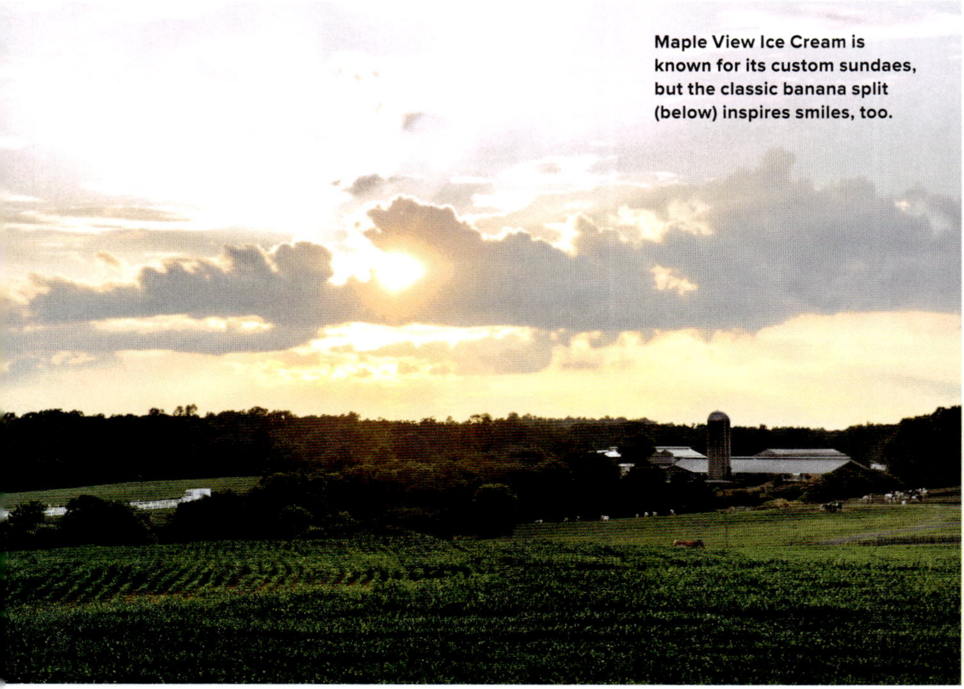

Maple View Ice Cream is known for its custom sundaes, but the classic banana split (below) inspires smiles, too.

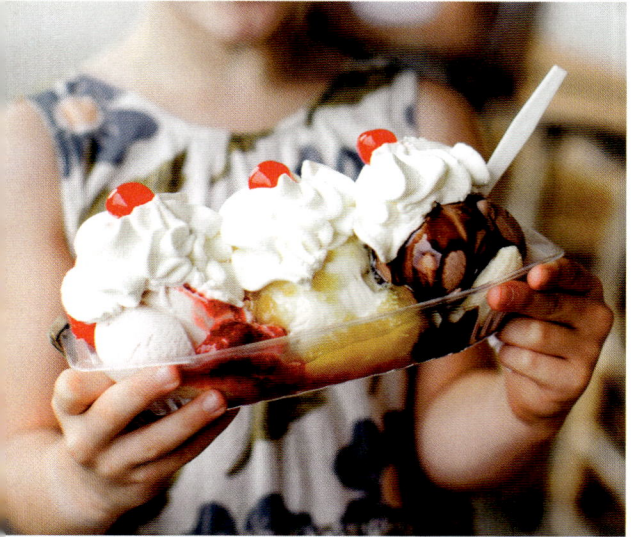

MAPLE VIEW ICE CREAM

Hillsborough

Finding your way to the rocker-lined front porch of Maple View Ice Cream is easy: Just follow the cyclists on surrounding country roads each weekend, zipping along in lines like ants to a picnic. They're drawn to this former dairy farm for sundaes, cones, and other treats made with products from Simply Natural Creamery in Ayden.

6900 Rocky Ridge Road
(919) 960-5535
mapleviewfarm.com

PHOTOGRAPHY BY ANNA ROUTH BARZIN, MATT RAY PHOTOGRAPHY

BURNEY'S SWEETS & MORE
Elizabethtown

A fried — and famed — croissant fresh from the kitchen practically glows under a halo of glaze — like a doughnut, but a little bit more everything. Crispier on the outside. Softer on the inside. And a more perfect vehicle for all kinds of fillings: cream cheese, chocolate, lemon, and blueberry.

**106 M.L.K. Drive
(910) 862-2099**
burneyssweetsandmore.com

SWEET PLACES | PIEDMONT

The Candy Factory
Lexington

It works like this: You walk into a store, and it's candy, all candy. You stand in front of tiers of tubs filled with saltwater taffies that your kids are stuffing into paper bags along with hard candies and chocolates. The folks who work the store are so kind that you feel safe. Some of the rest of your life melts away. You try to show your sons a hard blue lozenge wrapped in cellophane. *These are what my grandmother had in that silver bowl in the front room*, you try to tell them. *We weren't allowed to eat them. We snuck them all the time.* Licorice Starlights. Peppermint Ice. Snappy Gingers. Peanut Butter Logs. Mary Janes. Butterscotch Buttons. Crystal Mints. Caramel Creams. "Candy store" doesn't do this landmark shop in Lexington justice: It's a time machine. — *Drew Perry*

15 North Main Street
(336) 249-6770, lexingtoncandyfactory.com

PHOTOGRAPHY BY JOEY SEAWELL

At The Candy Factory, cases are filled with fudge and chocolates, and bins brim with sweets that adults will remember from childhood.

SWEET PLACES EASTERN

Mickey's Pastry Shop
Goldsboro

Melanie Daniel's starter dough is older than she is. It was a gift from her father, who received it from his father-in-law, Mickey McClenny. Mickey received it in 1946, when he bought the bakery from Nathan Crocker, who opened his bakery in downtown Goldsboro in 1920. More than 75 years later, Melanie continues Mickey's legacy by baking lemon squares with scattered constellations of sugar on top, cream horns and long johns, her grandfather's buttercream-topped cakes, and dozens of other pastries. Some, like the long johns and cream puffs, begin with the ancient starter. Others have different ingredients, but still begin with one of Mickey's beloved recipes.

— *Eleanor Spicer Rice*

2704 Graves Drive
(919) 759-4741, mickeyspastry.com

Mickey's cinnamon buns rarely make it through the morning rush, while buttercream-frosted cupcakes are a perfect treat at any time of day.

PHOTOGRAPHY BY STACEY VAN BERKEL

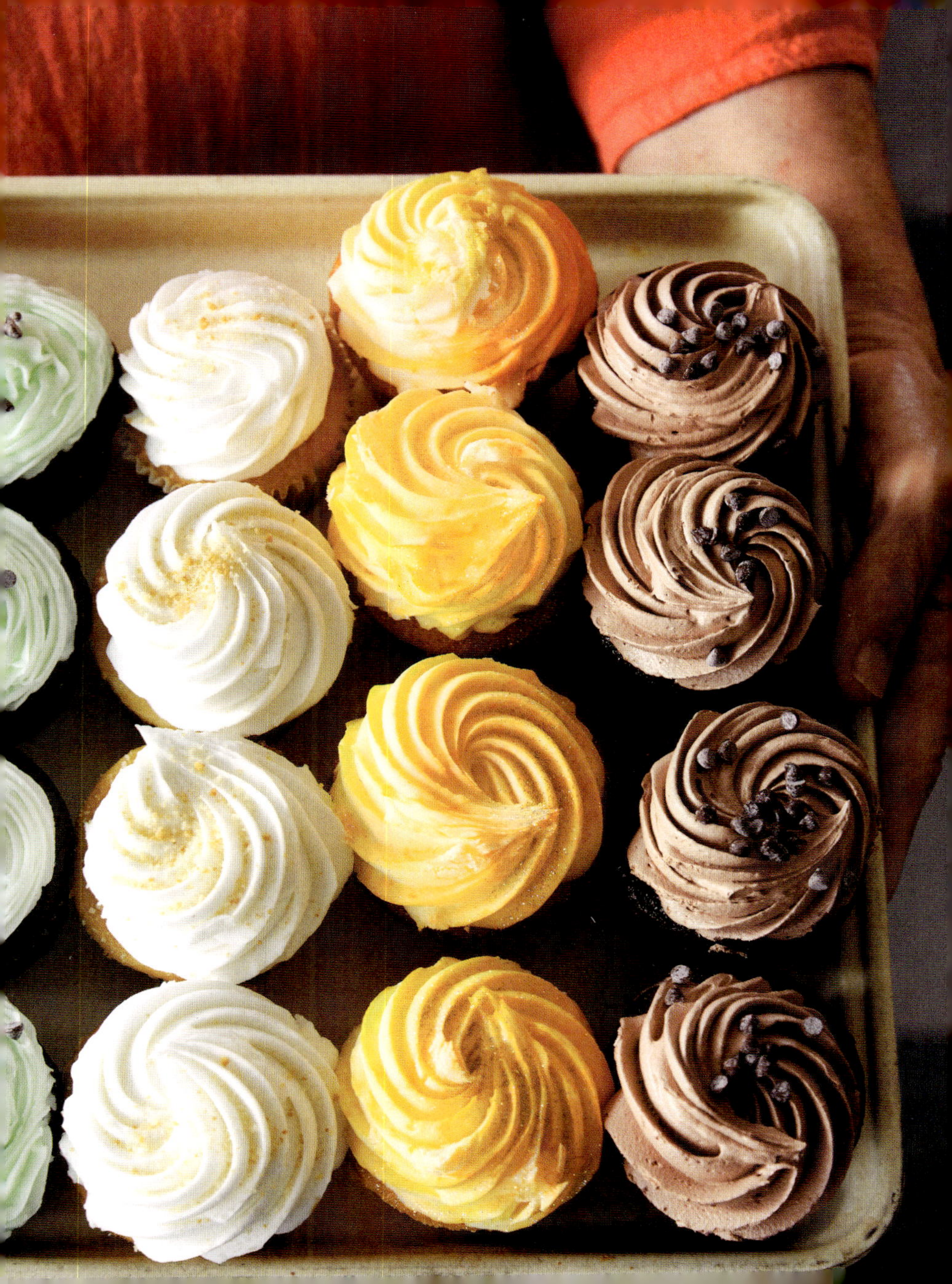

SWEET PLACES EASTERN

The Peppered Cupcake
Wilmington

At Tabitha Meready's downtown Wilmington shop, magically light, smooth buttercream is the crowning glory on moist cupcakes in flavors like peach-and-lavender cobbler, jalapeño-strawberry shortcake, bourbon pecan pie, and banana pudding.

But for her signature cupcakes, inspired by a family recipe for Jezebel sauce, Meready stuffs vanilla cupcakes with a preserve of the day, frosts them, then adds a spoonful of mango-chili or peach-habanero pepper jelly on top for a sweet-and-spicy surprise.

— *Katie Schanze*

**105 South Front Street
(910) 399-1088, thepepperedcupcake.com**

SUNSET SLUSH
Ocean Isle Beach

Since 2004, Sunset Slush's pushcarts have patrolled Ocean Isle Beach and Oak Island, luring customers with their wide variety of sweet and refreshing Italian ices (right).

6848 Beach Drive Southwest
sunsetslush.com

Try a one-of-a-kind pepper jelly cupcake in Wilmington (opposite). At Ocean Isle Beach, keep your eyes peeled for the original Sunset Slush pushcart (above).

SWEET PLACES EASTERN

BRITTS DONUT SHOP
Carolina Beach

Since 1939, there's been a line out the door. The Carolina Beach Boardwalk has gone through its share of changes, but at least one thing about it has stood the test of time: the "Sweetest Place on Earth" and its warm, made-from-scratch, raised doughnuts with a flaky glaze. Served warm on a wax paper rectangle, or in a white paper bag, these tender, glazed confections make the expression "melt-in-your-mouth" a reality.

1 Carolina Beach Avenue North
(910) 707-0755, brittsdonutshop.com

CELTIC CREAMERY
Carolina Beach

In a seaside town in Ireland, Jeff Hogan tasted the best ice cream he'd ever had. It was creamy and dense — with more butterfat and less air than the ice cream he was used to. He spent the next several years trying to convince the shop owner, Joanna McCarthy, to let him bring her recipe to the United States. Eventually she agreed, and in 2018, Celtic Creamery began serving a taste of Ireland on Carolina shores.

201 North Lake Park Boulevard
(910) 707-0943, celticcreamery.com

| SWEET PLACES | EASTERN

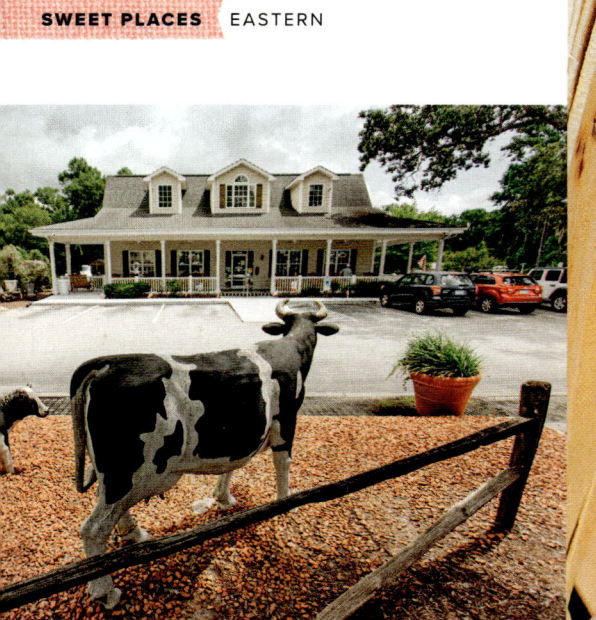

Calabash Creamery
Calabash

They arrive in Calabash from all over — locals and tourists trolling for seafood dinners. Then they ease over to Calabash Creamery for a sugary finish. Yes, the "Seafood Capital of the World" also has a sweet spot. Most customers take their old-fashioned ice cream out to the porch to rock and watch the line of traffic from Calabash to the nearby beaches: Sunset, Ocean Isle, and Myrtle. No one hurries. And why would they? After all, they've topped their seafood feast with a scoop (or three) of creamy sweetness. That's a taste, and a moment, worth savoring. — *Tim Bass*

9910 Beach Drive Southwest
(910) 575-1180, calabashcreamery.com

At Calabash Creamery, Sunset Peach ice cream — made with local peaches — is a seasonal favorite.

SURFIN' SPOON
Nags Head

This shop owned by Jesse and Whitney Hines — a professional surfer and an artist — is known for its amazing frozen yogurt and its creative ice cream sandwiches.

3408 South Virginia Dare Trail
(252) 441-7873, surfinspoon.com

RACHEL K's BAKERY
Washington

Inside a historic 1884 building that once served as town hall, you'll find carrot cake, oatmeal cream pies, brownies, cinnamon buns, and more — treats dreamed up by longtime baker Rachel Midgette.

126 North Market Street
(252) 946-2253
rachelksbakery.com

THE FUDGEBOAT
Carolina Beach

More than 40 flavors of homemade fudge are displayed in an old boat that washed up on the beach during a hurricane. For a real treat, order a scoop of homemade ice cream with melted fudge drizzled over the top.

107 Carolina Beach Avenue North
(910) 458-5823
fudgeboat.com

SWEET PLACES EASTERN

The slogan at Becky Williams's bakery declares, "It's all about the buttercream," as evidenced by the intricate flowers and other decorations that top many of her cakes.

PHOTOGRAPHY BY ANNA ROUTH BARZIN, CHRIS HANNANT

CAKES BY BECKY
Williamston

The cakes that Becky Williams had been decorating from her home became legendary through word of mouth: unicorn birthday cakes, wedding cakes with floral cascades, and party squares topped with wee baby bootees. Her kitchen was constantly smeared with multicolored buttercreams and speckled with sprinkles. Now, Williams's country bakery has counter space for her to decorate up to 20 custom cakes each week and allows customers to pop in for seasonal cupcakes and cookies.

118 Harrison Street
(252) 789-1922
facebook.com/cakesbybecky

ORANGE BLOSSOM BAKERY & CAFÉ
Buxton

The bevy of barefoot beachgoers at the counter is growing. Long-haired surfers in swim trunks and sleepy vacationers in cover-ups stand in a line that winds out the door, across the front porch, and down the ramp to the parking lot. They're all waiting for Apple Uglies. The three-pound mess of hot, doughy, apple-cinnamon goodness isn't pretty — hence the name — but that doesn't matter when it goes straight from bag to hand to mouth.

47206 NC Highway 12
orangeblossombakery.com

SWEET PLACES

JARS *of* JOY

Bread's best friend isn't butter (unless you're talking about the apple kind). That honor belongs to sweet, seasonal fruit picked fresh and preserved in all its smashed, jammed, and jellied glory.

GARNET GALS
Andrews

Garnet Spencer passed down her love of preserves to her daughter and granddaughter, Andrea and Megan Lambert. Now, the Lamberts carry on her traditions with their business named in her honor.

garnetgals.com

MRS. RUTH'S JAMS
Apex

Ruth Taylor started out making jam for her friends and family. In addition to offering signature flavors like Belgian chocolate strawberry and blueberry orange, Taylor often collaborates with customers to re-create childhood memories or family recipes.

mrsruthsjams.com

WILDFLOUR BAKERY
Gloucester

In the Whites' home bakery, Gary makes the baked goods, and Cathy makes the jam to spread on top. The couple sells sweet treats like whiskey fig cakes and scrumptious spreads like strawberry margarita jam and pear rosemary preserves at the Olde Beaufort Farmers Market.

(252) 241-1581
facebook.com/wildflourbakeryjams

IMLADRIS FARM
Fairview

Imladris Farm has been in the same family for seven generations, and Walter and Wendy Harrill are dedicated to sustainable agriculture and production to maintain their family's legacy. They grow their own berries and purchase fruit from other local mountain farms to create timeless classics like blackberry, blueberry, and raspberry jams.

imladrisfarm.com

BLUE RIDGE JAMS
Hendersonville

Linda Justice opened The Sugar Shack in 1961, and it's been in the family ever since. Current owners Robin and Steve Pridmore changed the name to Blue Ridge Jams for wholesale to local shops and restaurants, but you can still find the Sugar Shack label at farmers markets in and around Hendersonville. Blue Ridge has around 120 flavors — crowd favorites include habanero raspberry and strawberry fig.

(828) 685-1783, blueridgejam.com

Garnet Gals

PHOTOGRAPHY BY ERIC WATERS, TIM ROBISON

Strawberry jelly, apricot jam, and sweet tomato preserves made by **Blue Ridge Jams** in Hendersonville are perfect on homemade biscuits.

SWEET STORIES

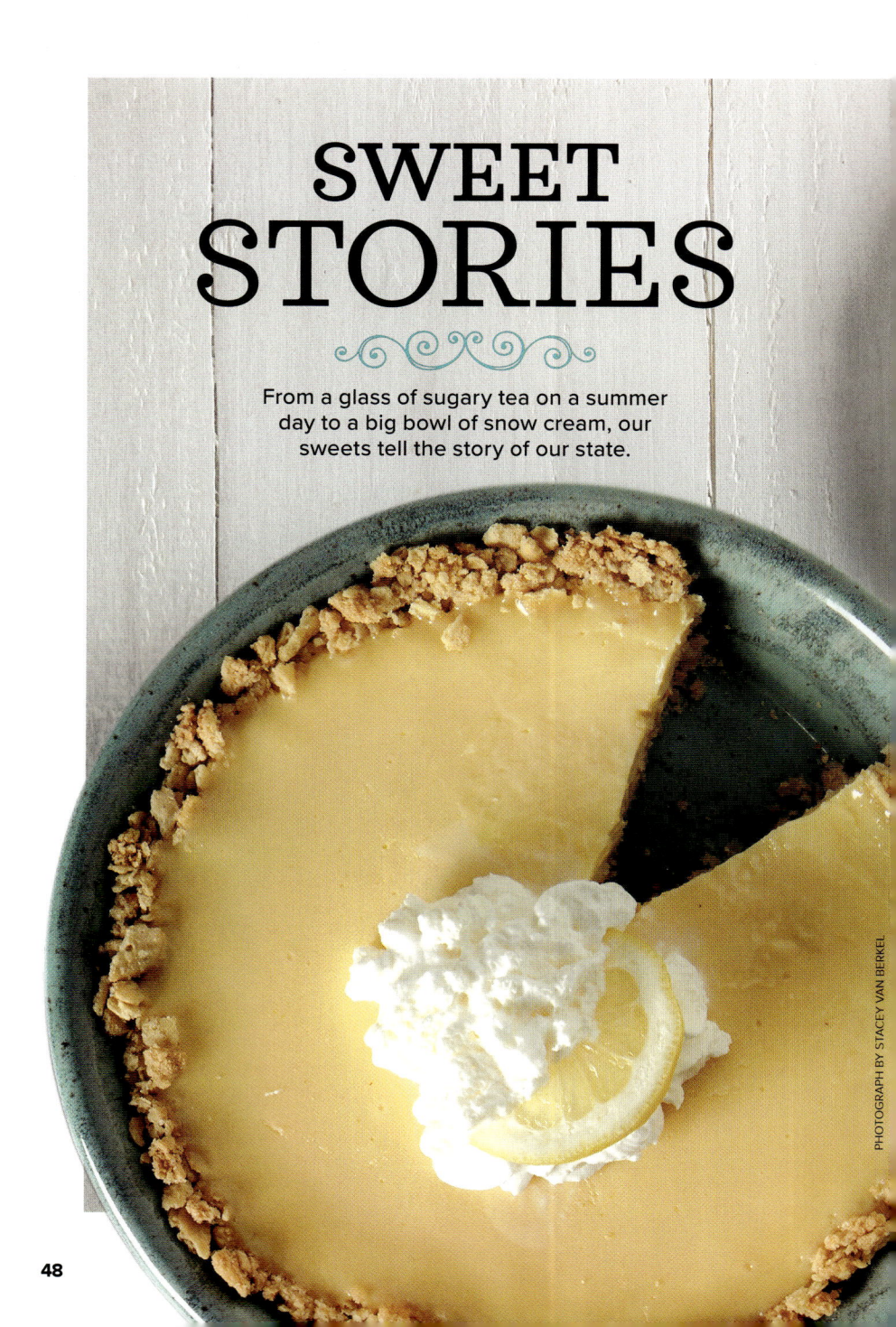

From a glass of sugary tea on a summer day to a big bowl of snow cream, our sweets tell the story of our state.

Atlantic Beach pie was a new creation based on an old tradition, with whipped cream and flaky salt instead of meringue, and a saltine crust instead of Ritz Crackers. For the recipe, see page 92.

SWEET STORIES

Atlantic Beach Pie

Chef Emeritus Bill Smith wanted to re-create the lemon pie of his childhood on the coast — with some tweaks. He called the dessert Atlantic Beach pie. It was a hit. Then it went viral. Now, it's legendary.

PHOTOGRAPH BY TIM ROBISON

When I was growing up in New Bern in the '50s, people believed as absolute truth that if you ate dessert after a meal of seafood, you would probably die. In the back of my mind, I thought that maybe this rule was just a way to trick me into eating fewer sweets. There was one exception, though: lemon pie.

If you asked why, you were told something about lemon and fish. Therefore, many seafood restaurants on North Carolina's coast served Atlantic Beach lemon pie, if no other dessert.

The best thing about the pie wasn't the lemon flavor, but its salty, cracker-crumb crust — made with Ritz or saltine crackers — which distinguished it from sweet piecrusts made with crushed cookies or graham crackers.

I remembered that pie when I was asked to teach a group of chefs and food writers from the Southern Foodways Alliance about eastern North Carolina's food traditions. After some research — a phone call here, an old church cookbook there — and some experimentation, I developed my version of the Atlantic Beach lemon pie.

The original had meringue, but I opted for whipped cream sprinkled with coarse sea salt. I crumbled saltine crackers for the crust. My recipe requires half a cup of lemon or lime juice, or a mix of both, and condensed milk. I served the pie to 600 Southern Foodways guests, and then brought the recipe back to my restaurant, Crook's Corner in Chapel Hill.

To my surprise, the pie became a sensation. Word of it eventually reached Melissa Gray, who has a series called "Found Recipes" that airs on NPR's "All Things Considered."

We did a segment together, and when the story aired on a Thursday, almost immediately my staff started saying that we were running out of Atlantic Beach pie.

The next day, my baker made more pies, but customers cleaned us out again. This went on all weekend.

And just when I thought the phenomenon of Atlantic Beach pie had subsided, I got an email from the Atlanta Food and Wine Festival. Could I make Atlantic Beach pie for 700 people? Of course.

This pie will be the death of me.

—*Bill Smith*

SWEET STORIES

In the Piedmont, Coastal Plain, and even some pockets of the mountains, snow is such an unexpected gift that there's only one way to properly celebrate it: snow cream.

PHOTOGRAPH BY MATT HULSMAN

Snow Cream

In a quest for the perfect bowl of snow cream, the sweetest spoonfuls are always found in the past.

◦◦◦◦◦◦◦

I grew up in Boone, a small town perched among the higher peaks of our Blue Ridge Mountains, a place that expects a few good snows each winter, or at least we did back then. Despite all that snow there for the taking, I recall making snow cream only once, after reading about it in a library book when I was in third grade.

Homemade snow cream is sweet and cold, nothing more than sugar, milk, vanilla, and snow stirred together, and nothing less than magic. It requires copious amounts of freshly fallen snow — which, in much of North Carolina, is a phenomenon as rare and fleeting as shooting stars, as I would come to learn. People don't make snow cream because they have a recipe; they make it because having

SWEET STORIES

> **Snow cream always turns out just right because it's magic in the first place.**

enough snow to make a batch is a special occasion.

My grandparents were game to help with my experiment, as grandparents often are. Mama Madge lent me her large enameled dishpan to harvest my snow. Daddy Fred went out with me because he was always up for my adventures. We trudged into the backyard, to a spot where the snow was still as smooth and soft as a freshly made feather bed. Daddy Fred held the pan while I scooped up heaping mittenfuls of snow.

Back in the house, Mama had gathered the sugar, milk — I'd bet my lunch money it was the canned milk she liked in her coffee — and vanilla. The yellow wooden step stool that brought me up to counter height was in place. I concocted a big batch with great flourish, stirring with a long-handled spoon. Mama scooped my handiwork into the brightly colored aluminum drinking cups we used for supper each night. I don't recall much about what that snow cream actually tasted like, but I'm certain it was perfectly delicious. Snow cream always turns out just right because it's magic in the first place.

Snow cream magic struck again about 30 years later. This time, I was the mama, and the snow cream connoisseur was my then 4-year-old daughter. I'd moved down off the mountain and was living in the flat land known as the Triangle, a place where measurable snow is rare. Due to a string of dry winters, my daughter had never seen more than a dusting. Newscasters predicted a whopper, but every North Carolinian knows that a snow forecast can be fickle. This time, it was accurate. Big, fat, feathery flakes started coming down overnight, and by morning, the ground was blanketed. I heard my footy-pajama-clad girl get out of bed and peek through the blinds into the backyard. She gasped with delight. Then I heard her run across the hall and look out another window. "Mama! Mama!" she exclaimed. "It snowed in the front yard, too!"

Snow cream doesn't need much to make it delicious.

That snow was one for the record books, something like 20 inches. We didn't have a sled, so I pulled out my largest baking pan, so big that she could sit on it with legs stretched out long.

Maybe snow cream came to mind because I knew there would be few snow days of that caliber in her childhood. Or maybe a snow angel whispered in my ear. Of course I pulled out Mama's dishpan and helped my daughter scoop up mittenfuls of snow. She and her sledding buddies tumbled inside and shed their winter wear near the door.

I put the dishpan of snow on the counter and slid chairs up to the edge so the little ones could reach. I handed each of them a cup to scoop some snow into the mixing bowl of vanilla-scented milk and sugar. Everyone got a turn to stir.

My daughter, now grown, can't recall what that snow cream tasted like, but she's certain it was perfectly delicious. Snow cream might be the sorriest ice cream you'll ever try, but it's guaranteed to be the best snow you'll ever eat. — *Sheri Castle*

SWEET STORIES

Moravian Cookies

Sometimes called the world's thinnest cookie, these sweet ginger snaps also offer a North Carolina history lesson.

If you want to study state history, the Moravian cookie is a good way to do so. In the 1700s, Moravians — a devout Christian denomination that originated around what is now Germany and the Czech Republic — settled in present-day Forsyth County and established a town, Salem.

In those days, small baked sweets were often called cakes. Since the Moravians had access to spices like ginger, black pepper, and allspice, as well as honey and molasses, they would make a thick, dark spice cookie, a form of German *lebkuchen*, that was stamped with elaborate designs using wooden rollers or molds. Made from a low-moisture dough that would keep longer, the sweets traveled well. By the mid-1800s, the word "cookie" came into style, along with leaveners like baking powder, which made cakes into something lighter and softer. Bakers began to roll out their dough much thinner, either to increase the yield or to bake faster in wood-fired ovens. They cut the dough into simple shapes, like circles and hearts, using tin cookie cutters.

These days, even lifelong Moravians rarely make Moravian cookies by hand anymore. Most prefer to buy them from storied Winston-Salem cookie companies. That's because they're notoriously difficult to make: The dough, traditionally flavored with warm spices like ginger, cloves, mace, and nutmeg is made in batches so large that they could defeat a cement mixer. Then, it has to be rolled out so thin that you can almost see through it — which means that cutting out and baking the cookies is particularly difficult, too. It seems that nothing about these beloved cookies comes easily — except, of course, eating them. — *Kathleen Purvis*

PHOTOGRAPH BY JOEY SEAWELL

Moravian cookies have a thickness you can measure in the width of a Keebler elf's eyelash. They're also crisp — if a potato chip were a cookie, it would be Moravian.

SWEET STORIES

Sweet Tea

We stir together a handful of humble ingredients to produce an amber elixir that tastes like the South and feels like home.

People divide the South from the North at the Mason-Dixon Line, but I've always thought the real marker is the sweet-tea line — the point where, at the next diner north, they don't have sweet tea ready to pour. I'm not sure just where the line is. I feel sorry for those poor souls up above it. But one thing's for sure: North Carolina is on the good side.

And over the years, in this part of the world, sweet tea has become infused with meaning. It's more than just a drink. Sweet tea is our alchemy — our gift of making something special from humble ingredients. Sweet tea is our love offering, poured for family and neighbors and even the guy trying to sell us new gutters. And at its most basic, sweet tea is a cold blast on a hot day, like a dip in a river from the inside out.

We've been drinking sweet tea down here for nearly two centuries now, although the tea of the early 1800s doesn't much resemble what most of us drink with cornbread and greens.

The two big events that converted the South to the sweet tea we know today were Prohibition, which got rid of (most of) the nation's alcohol, and ice delivery, which gave people a way to cool down a big glass. By the 1930s, sweet iced tea was as common at the Carolina table as salt and pepper shakers.

You can buy sweet tea all over the country now, way past the sweet-tea line. But what we're talking about, when we talk about sweet tea, is something brewed that morning, stirred by hand, served by a waitress who calls you darlin', poured out of one of those special pitchers with the spout on the side, or better yet, sitting in the fridge at your mama's house. — *Tommy Tomlinson*

PHOTOGRAPH BY STACEY VAN BERKEL

Even within the simple sweet-tea trinity — tea bags, sugar, water — there are all kinds of variations.

SWEET STORIES

There's nothing more American than apple pie — except maybe enjoying a slice in an old-fashioned diner.

60

Diner Pie

In a glass case by the door, or on a dessert plate in an old-school booth, few foods evoke as strong a sense of place as coffee's favorite companion: a slice of diner pie.

Reader, indulge me for a moment, and think about diner pie. Contemplate it. Lately, I've been doing that a lot. I've been taking the subject of diner pie very seriously, because it intrigues me. Because what *is* diner pie, really? This is the only question that needs to be asked, that needs to be answered. Can it be known and defined — *can it be understood* — the way corn can be understood, for instance, or chicken, or even a barbecue sandwich?

Let's break it down into its constituent parts, like the amateur culinary anthropologists we are.

Diner. Diners are romantic, mostly bygone, reminiscent of the 1950s, and as nostalgic as ducktails and lunchtime martinis. These days, it seems, any joint that serves breakfast past noon can call itself a diner, but a diner is so much more than that. A diner looks like an abandoned Art Deco train car with a counter running through it, with either one big jukebox near the swinging door to the kitchen or 50 tiny jukeboxes, one at each booth, plus a waitress named Flo and a short-order cook smoking a cigar. Other than drive-in theaters and cowboys, there is nothing more American than a diner.

Pie. I do not need to explain what pie is to anybody because all of us are born with an idea of pie in our baby brains. Pie is a sign that you're actually alive and living in

SWEET STORIES

Coconut custard pie has been on the menu since the '50s at Blake's Restaurant in Candor.

what's known as civilization. The next time we send an unmanned probe into space to look for intelligent life, we should put a pie inside of it, because pie is *the* universal language.

But it becomes more complicated when you put the two words together. *Diner pie.* Diner plus pie creates an entirely new thing in the world. I know of no other food as specific as this: one that can only be what it is by being served in a particular place.

Here are some facts. There are five standard diner pies: apple, blueberry, cherry, chocolate, and lemon meringue — like The Beatles, if you count Pete Best. Slices used to be displayed on diner counters, in rotating cylindrical cases — and sometimes still are — but that's rare these days. A big question in the world of diner pies is whether it can even be called a diner pie without the cylindrical case. Another is, can you really say you've eaten a piece of diner pie if it

> **Can you really say you've eaten a piece of diner pie if it didn't come with a cup of thick black coffee on the side?**

didn't come with a cup of thick black coffee on the side? And must the pie be at least one day old (*atmospheric marination*, I call that), or can it be eaten fresh from the oven?

When is diner pie just ... pie?

How we think about food raises some of the most fundamental questions of how we understand the world. I love the specificity of diner pie. I would like other foods to be that specific. Because if we were to apply diner pie logic to the rest of the food we eat, we would have a very particular locality associated with all of it: Church Beans. Locker Room Grilled Cheese. Supply Closet Mashed Potatoes. Late for Work Eggs. Et cetera. This is what Diner Pie reminds us, what it teaches us: that it's not simply *what* we eat, but *where* we eat it that's important. A diner is to pie what home is to a home-cooked meal: You won't find either anywhere else.

— *Daniel Wallace*

SWEET STORIES

Banana Pudding

This simple dish is built in layers, rich and comforting, reflecting the foundation of a satisfying Southern life.

There's no point in looking for the best banana pudding in North Carolina. Styrofoam-cupped, 95-cent, vending-machine banana pudding is good. Truck-stop-diner, skin-on-top, three-day-old banana pudding is good. You don't search for the best banana pudding. You just search for banana pudding. The best is what's in front of you.

This is what makes banana pudding the signature Southern food. Nobody argues much over banana pudding. Make it however you want. Just save me some.

We should probably stop right here, just in case you're visiting from Saskatchewan and you don't know banana pudding. It's simple. One, slice some bananas. Two, mix up some vanilla pudding — yes, it sounds like you should use banana flavor, but roll with it. Three, get you a box of vanilla wafers. That's the holy trinity. Some people add whipped cream. Others make a meringue. A few grind nutmeg over the top. You'll even find recipes that substitute ladyfingers for the vanilla wafers. There are many ways to gild a lily.

The only rule is this: Banana pudding is made in layers. Bananas, pudding, wafers, repeat. Banana pudding is geology. Over time — and it doesn't take long — the layers press together. The flavors seep into one another. With every bite, you can taste not only the ingredients but also what they have melded into, creamy and cool, with just enough resistance for your tongue to push up against.

Layers of taste. Layers of time. And, sometimes, layers of love. — *Tommy Tomlinson*

PHOTOGRAPH BY MATT HULSMAN

Few North Carolinians can agree on who makes the best barbecue, but we all agree that it should be chased with a dish of banana pudding.

SWEET STORIES

Ice Cream

Old-fashioned churns are about working together: Each turn of the crank brings us all one step closer to sweet, frozen bliss.

I got married in a time when people still received ice cream churns as wedding gifts. Ours is electric. Electric is fine, and it's not cheating, but it misses the point. Churning ice cream should be an enterprise of many, one of those group efforts that prove that if you work hard, and wait, something good comes of it. If a machine is mindlessly humming away in the kitchen, like the rock tumbler that ground for weeks under my son's bed, the results are less appreciated.

As a child, I lacked muscles, patience, and any capacity for chemistry, but I was fascinated by the dripping, glistening, silvery cylinder pulled — with effort — from the churn. There was ice cream inside that thing? How? The grown-ups referred to a "dasher" and a "paddle," but this metal

The best-tasting peach ice cream requires a little effort.

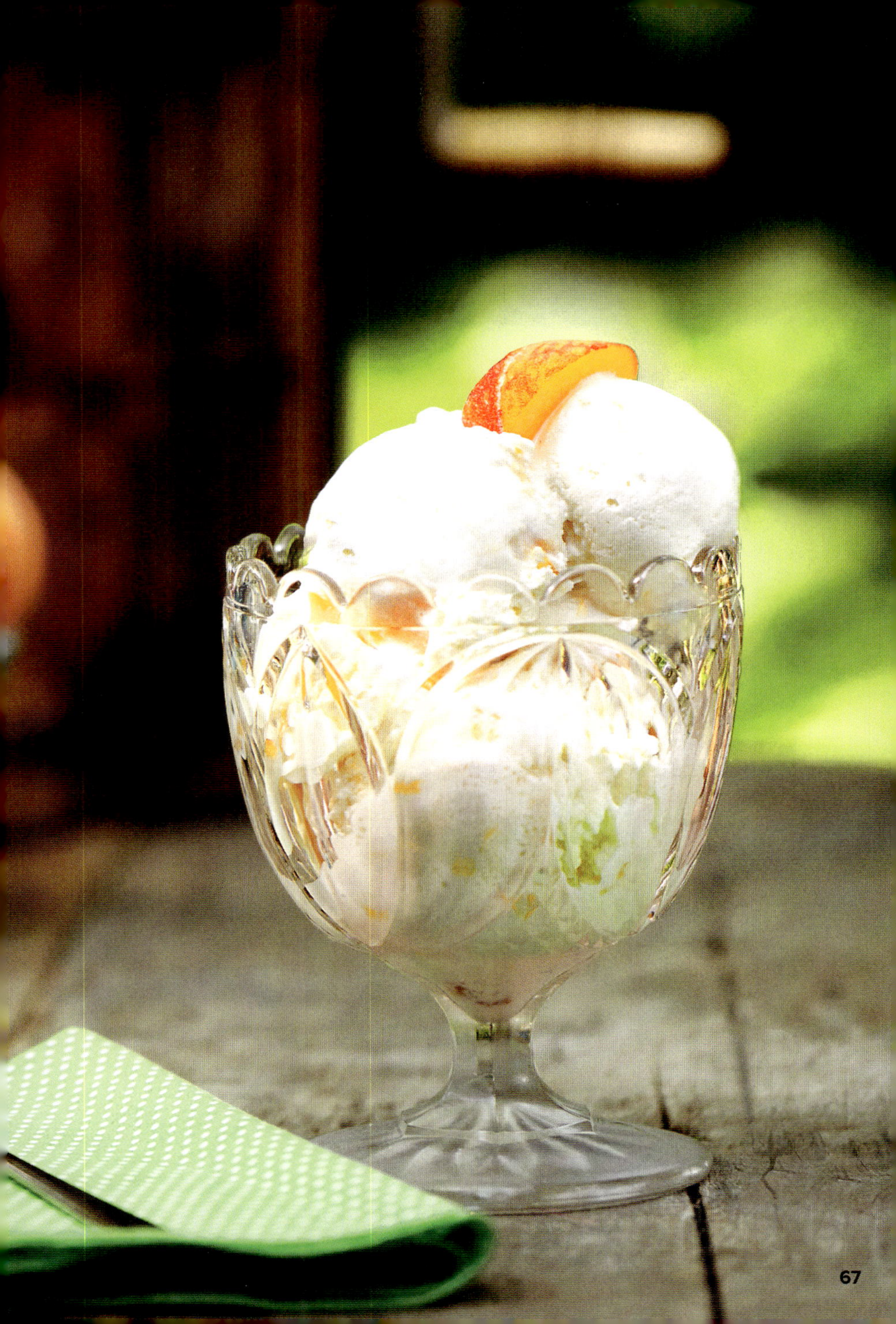

SWEET STORIES

To be authentic and American, Southern and summery, find yourself a wooden ice cream churn.

wedge looked somewhat lethal; certainly nothing like one of Santa's reindeer or a canoe oar. What did salt, of all things, have to do with sugary ice cream? And *rock* salt ... was that like the rock candy that I made on a string dangling in sugar water?

Actually, I still don't get it: *As salt melts the ice, the heat of fusion allows the ice to absorb heat from the ice cream mixture, which freezes the ice cream.* Apparently, it's all about aerating, but ... who cares? And who cares that it's never as creamy as commercial brands, but a granular, just-this-side-of-icy, snow-cream texture? You eat churned ice cream with a plastic spoon from a paper cup or cardboard bowl 'cause there are so many folks around for the reunion or birthday or holiday or just a Sunday supper. And you eat it fast, 'cause hand-churned ice cream melts fast.

Doesn't matter that the scoop dotted with peach or strawberry or peppermint bits — don't attempt chocolate; just let Dairy Queen have the rights — can't stand up to butterscotch or chocolate syrup. Doesn't matter that you might taste the teeniest bit of salt along with the fruity or minty flavor; that's what makes cranked cream the real thing.

Yes, yes, yes. There are a jillion ways,

available on the Internet, to make ice cream in your freezer now, or some version of it. I love my mother-in-law's recipe for lemon ice, with lemonade mixed into melty, then refrozen, (commercial) vanilla ice cream.

But to be authentic and American and simultaneously Southern and summery, find yourself a wooden ice cream churn. Then find rock salt in the grocery store. Good luck with that. You'll need a porch, a carport, a back stoop, or level ground beneath a tree, because churning needs to be done outside, and it's work. Hot work. Churners need shade. Churners also need lawn chairs. (Look at an ice cream churn. No one churns standing up.) Gather friends, kin, and bicep braggers; assign shifts; and enjoy that comforting *crunkleshumm* noise, a slurry-ish sound of the nicest sort. Let someone else figure out what to do with the salty water.

Quit the crank. Extract the dasher. Take a spatula to the sides. Spoon it up. Regard the lowly ice cream churn and realize, once again, that something you have to work for makes enjoying it all the sweeter.

— *Susan Stafford Kelly*

SWEET RECIPES

Satisfy your sweet tooth with some of our most irresistible — and iconic — desserts.

Fried Apple Pies

Yield: 12 servings.

- ½ stick unsalted butter
- 3 tablespoons brown sugar
- 2 cups Granny Smith apples, peeled, cored, and chopped (about 2-3 apples, depending on size)
- 2 tablespoons lemon juice
- ¼ teaspoon salt
- ¼ teaspoon ground nutmeg
- ½ teaspoon ground cinnamon
- 1 egg yolk
- ½ cup ice water
- 1 package (2 crusts) premade piecrust
- ½ cup all-purpose flour
- 2 cups vegetable oil, for frying
- Powdered sugar or granulated sugar, for dusting (optional)

In a saucepan, melt the butter and brown sugar together; add chopped apples, lemon juice, and salt. Simmer covered, over medium heat, for 15 to 20 minutes. Remove from heat and stir in nutmeg and cinnamon. Set aside to cool.

Mix egg yolk with ice water and set aside.

Place premade piecrust onto a floured surface and sprinkle more flour on top, working it into the dough. Roll out to about ⅛-inch thickness and cut into 6-inch circles. Place 2 teaspoons of the cooled filling in the center of each round. Lightly brush the edges of the dough with the egg wash, fold over, and gently press down on the edges and the filling. Seal the edges with the tines of a fork. Place the pies in a single layer onto a plate that has been lightly sprinkled with flour and refrigerate for 15 minutes.

In a skillet or Dutch oven, heat oil to 375°. Carefully drop 2 to 3 pies at a time into hot oil to avoid a drop in temperature. Fry for about 3 minutes or until pies turn golden brown on both sides. Use tongs to remove pies from the skillet, drain on paper towels, and sprinkle with granulated sugar or dust with powdered sugar, if desired.

— *Lynn Wells*

71

Strawberry Icebox Cake

Yield: 16 servings.

CAKE:
- 1 package moist white cake mix
- 1 cup vegetable oil
- 1 (3-ounce) package strawberry-flavored gelatin
- 4 large eggs, at room temperature
- ½ cup whole milk
- ½ cup chopped strawberries

FROSTING:
- ½ cup butter, softened
- 1 (1-pound) package powdered sugar
- ¾ cup chopped strawberries and their juice

WHIPPED TOPPING:
- 2 cups heavy cream, very cold
- 3 tablespoons powdered sugar
- 1 cup chopped strawberries

For the cake: Preheat oven to 350°. In a large bowl, combine cake mix, oil, and gelatin. Add eggs one at a time, alternating with milk and beating well after each addition. Fold in chopped strawberries. Pour into a greased 9 x 13-inch baking dish.

Bake for 45 to 55 minutes or until a toothpick comes out clean. Remove cake from oven and let cool in pan completely. Remove cake from pan. Using a serrated knife, slice cake in half horizontally.

For the frosting: In the bowl of an electric mixer, cream butter and sugar; add strawberries and just enough juice to reach a spreadable consistency. If strawberries have not produced enough juice, water may be added.

For the whipped topping: Using an electric mixer, whip cold heavy cream for 1 to 2 minutes until it begins to thicken. Add powdered sugar and continue to mix on low speed to form stiff peaks.

To assemble: Place one cake layer on a serving tray or baking dish. Cover with half of the frosting, then spread half of the whipped topping over frosting. Place ½ cup chopped strawberries on top. Repeat process with the second cake layer. Sprinkle remaining chopped strawberries over top layer of whipped topping. Cover with plastic wrap and refrigerate for at least 8 hours or overnight. — *Lynn Wells*

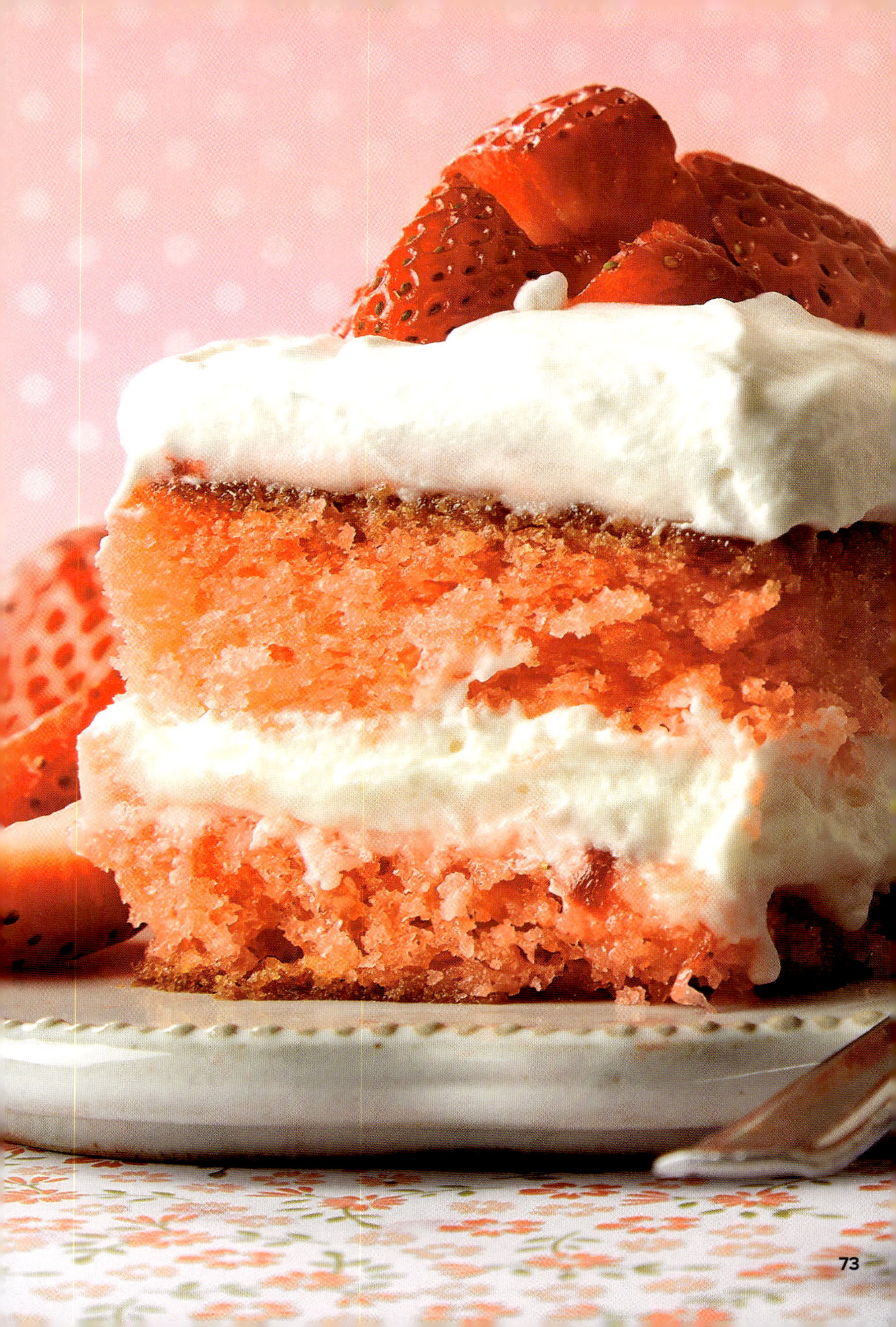

SWEET RECIPES

Strawberry Sonker with Dip

Yield: 12 servings.

PASTRY:
- 3 cups all-purpose flour
- ½ teaspoon salt
- 1 cup vegetable shortening
- 1 large egg
- 2 tablespoons distilled white vinegar
- 2 tablespoons butter, melted
- 3 tablespoons sugar

FILLING:
- 1 cup sugar
- ½ cup all-purpose flour
- ½ teaspoon ground cinnamon
- ¼ teaspoon ground nutmeg
- 1 cup water
- ½ cup (1 stick) butter, melted
- 8 cups fresh strawberries, halved or quartered if large

DIP:
- ½ cup sugar
- 3 tablespoons cornstarch
- Pinch of salt
- 3 cups whole milk
- ½ teaspoon vanilla extract

For the pastry: Whisk together the flour and salt in a large bowl. Work in the shortening with a pastry blender or fingertips until the mixture is crumbly.

Whisk together the egg and vinegar in a small bowl. Make a well in the center of the flour mixture, pour in the egg mixture, and stir with a fork to form soft dough that pulls in all of the dry ingredients. Form two balls, one using about ⅓ of the dough and the other using what's left. Place each ball on a sheet of plastic wrap, flatten to a disk about 1 inch thick, wrap well, and refrigerate for at least 3 hours, or up to overnight.

Position a rack in the center of the oven and preheat to 375°. Lightly grease a 9 x 13-inch baking pan.

For the filling: Whisk together the sugar, flour, cinnamon, and nutmeg in a large bowl. Whisk in the water and butter until smooth. Gently stir in the strawberries.

To assemble: Using lightly floured fingertips, press the larger disk of dough evenly across the bottom and up the sides of the prepared pan. Bake until the pastry is dry to the touch, but not browned, about 10 minutes. Pour in the strawberry mixture.

To make a lattice top crust, roll the other piece of dough on a lightly floured work surface into a 13x4-inch rectangle. Starting on one long side, use a pizza cutter to cut 4 long strips of dough that are 1 inch wide; arrange them lengthwise over the filling, spacing them evenly. Starting on a short side, cut the remaining dough crosswise into strips of dough that are 1 inch wide; arrange them perpendicular to the long strips of pastry, spacing them evenly to make a lattice. Brush the pastry with melted butter and sprinkle with sugar.

Bake until the pastry is deep golden brown and the filling bubbles, 45 to 50 minutes. Let cool on a wire rack for at least 15 minutes before serving. Meanwhile, make the dip.

For the dip: Whisk together the sugar, cornstarch, and salt in a medium saucepan. Whisk in the milk until smooth. Cook over medium heat, stirring until the mixture thickens enough to coat the spatula, about 5 minutes. Remove the pan from the heat and stir in the vanilla.

To serve, scoop warm sonker into serving bowls. Ladle a little warm dip over the top and serve at once. — *Sheri Castle*

75

SWEET RECIPES

Dark Chocolate Mocha Cherry Cookies

Yield: About 30 cookies.

- 1 **cup + 1 tablespoon all-purpose flour**
- ½ **teaspoon salt**
- ½ **teaspoon baking soda**
- ½ **cup unsalted butter, softened**
- ½ **cup packed light brown sugar**
- ½ **cup granulated sugar**
- ½ **teaspoon vanilla extract**
- 1 **large egg**
- 2 **teaspoons espresso powder or instant coffee, divided**
- 8 **ounces (1 cup) dark chocolate morsels**
- 1 **cup dried cherries, chopped**

Preheat oven to 350°. In a large bowl, whisk together flour, salt, and baking soda.

In the bowl of an electric mixer, cream butter and sugars until light and fluffy. Add vanilla, egg, and 1 teaspoon espresso powder; beat until creamy.

Beat in flour mixture, then stir in chocolate morsels and cherries. Drop dough by rounded teaspoons onto a parchment-lined cookie sheet. Bake for 10 to 12 minutes or until cookie edges are slightly browned and the centers are slightly soft. Dust cookies with remaining espresso powder. Cool on wire rack. — *Lynn Wells*

Chocolate Chess Pie

Yield: 8 servings.

- ½ cup salted butter, melted
- 1 cup sugar
- 4 tablespoons cocoa powder
- 3 eggs
- 1 (5-ounce) can evaporated milk
- 1 teaspoon vanilla extract
- 1 (9-inch) deep-dish pie shell (unbaked)
- Whipped cream (optional)

Preheat oven to 325°. In a bowl, combine butter, sugar, cocoa, eggs, evaporated milk, and vanilla. Mix well. Pour the mixture into the pie shell and spread it evenly along the edges. Bake for 45 minutes. Serve with whipped cream, if desired.

— *Lynn Wells*

Chocolate Cream Cheese Pound Cake

Yield: 16 servings.

CAKE:
- 1 pound unsalted butter, softened
- 3 cups sugar
- 8 ounces cream cheese, softened
- 6 large eggs
- 3 cups all-purpose flour
- ½ cup dark cocoa powder
- ½ teaspoon salt
- 1 teaspoon baking powder
- ½ cup whole milk, warm
- 1 teaspoon vanilla extract

CHOCOLATE ROYAL ICING:
- 4 cups powdered sugar
- ½ cup dark cocoa powder
- 2 egg whites, beaten
- 1 teaspoon vanilla extract
- ¾ cup + 2 tablespoons heavy cream

For the cake: Preheat oven to 325°. Butter, cream cheese, and eggs should be at room temperature. Cream together butter, sugar, and cream cheese until light and fluffy. Add eggs one at a time, beating well after each addition. In a bowl, combine flour, cocoa, salt, and baking powder. Add alternately with milk to creamed mixture, beginning and ending with dry ingredients. Stir in vanilla. Pour into greased and floured tube pan. Bake for 1 hour and 20 minutes, or until a toothpick inserted into the center comes out clean. Remove the cake from the oven and cover with foil until completely cool.

For the chocolate royal icing: In a mixing bowl, combine dry ingredients and mix lightly. In a separate bowl, mix egg whites, vanilla extract, and half of the cream. Add to the dry ingredients. With an electric mixer, mix on low speed, and gradually add the remaining cream. Mix until the icing reaches the consistency of thick syrup. Turn the mixer to high and whip for approximately 2 minutes, until the icing is light and fluffy, like meringue.

— *Lynn Wells*

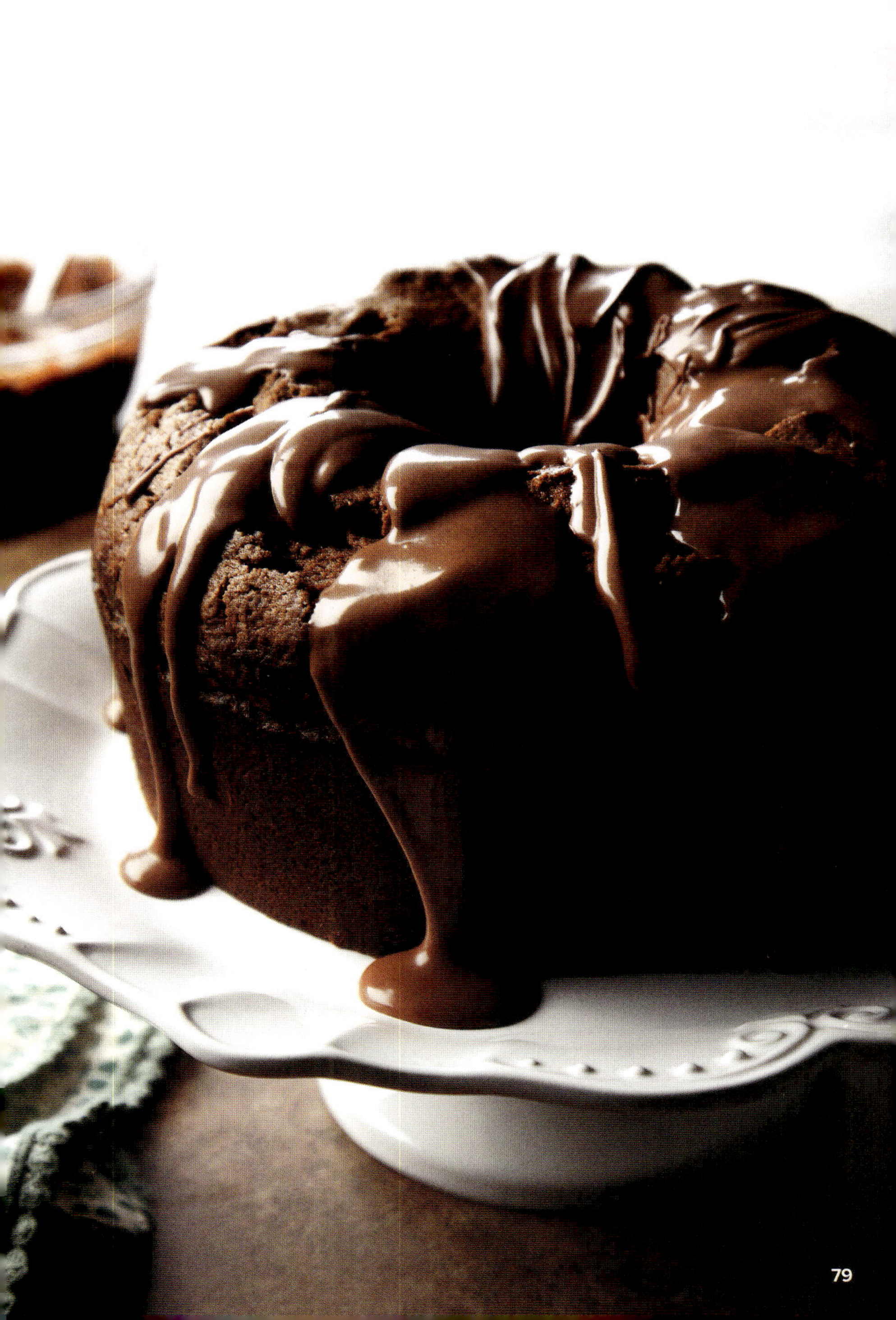

SWEET RECIPES

80

Black Walnut Hummingbird Cake

Yield: 12 servings.

CAKE:
- 3 cups all-purpose flour
- 2 cups sugar
- 1 teaspoon salt
- 1 teaspoon baking soda
- 1 teaspoon ground cinnamon
- ½ teaspoon freshly grated nutmeg
- 3 large eggs, beaten
- 1½ cups vegetable oil
- 1½ teaspoons vanilla extract
- 1 (8-ounce) can crushed pineapple, undrained
- 2 cups diced bananas (see note)
- 1 cup chopped black walnuts

CREAM CHEESE FROSTING:
- 1 pound cream cheese, at room temperature
- 1 cup (2 sticks) butter, softened
- 1 pound powdered sugar, sifted
- 2 teaspoons vanilla extract
- ½ cup black walnut pieces

For the cake: Heat the oven to 350°. Grease (with shortening) and flour three 9-inch round cake pans.

Whisk together the flour, sugar, salt, baking soda, cinnamon, and nutmeg in a large bowl. Add the eggs and oil, and stir only until the dry ingredients disappear into the batter; do not beat. Stir in the vanilla, pineapple, bananas, and walnuts.

Divide the batter among the cake pans. Gently tap the pans on the counter to remove air bubbles.

Bake until a wooden pick inserted in center comes out clean, 25 to 30 minutes. Place the pans on wire racks to cool for 10 minutes. Turn out the layers and cool completely on the wire racks for 1 hour.

For the frosting: In a large bowl, beat the cream cheese and butter until smooth with an electric mixer at medium speed. Gradually add the powdered sugar, beating at low speed until light and fluffy. Quickly beat in the vanilla.

Spread 1 cup of frosting between the cake layers, stacking them as you go. (For the most attractive layer cake, place the first cake layer bottom-side up and place the final cake layer top-side up.) Spread the remaining frosting over the top and around the sides of the cake. Pat walnuts over the top. Store refrigerated in an airtight cake carrier.

Note: The bananas are diced, not mashed. For the best texture and flavor, use ripe bananas that are evenly freckled with brown spots.

— *Sheri Castle*

SWEET RECIPES

Coconut Cream Pie

Yield: *8 servings.*

- 1 **cup unsweetened flaked coconut, lightly toasted**
- 1 **(9-inch) pie shell, baked and cooled**
- 2 **cups half-and-half**
- 1 **cup heavy cream**
- 3 **large eggs, room temperature, beaten**
- ¾ **cup sugar**
- ½ **cup all-purpose flour**
- 2 **tablespoons cornstarch**
- ½ **teaspoon salt**
- 1 **teaspoon vanilla extract**
- ½ **teaspoon coconut extract**
- 2 **cups whipped topping**

Preheat oven to 350°. In a medium saucepan, combine the half-and-half, heavy cream, eggs, sugar, flour, cornstarch, and salt. Whisk ingredients to mix well. Bring to a boil over medium heat, stirring constantly. Once the mixture begins to boil, continue stirring and cook for 2 minutes more. Remove from heat and stir in extracts. Let filling cool about 20 minutes. Pour filling into the pie shell and chill, uncovered, overnight. Top with whipped topping and toasted coconut.

— *Lynn Wells*

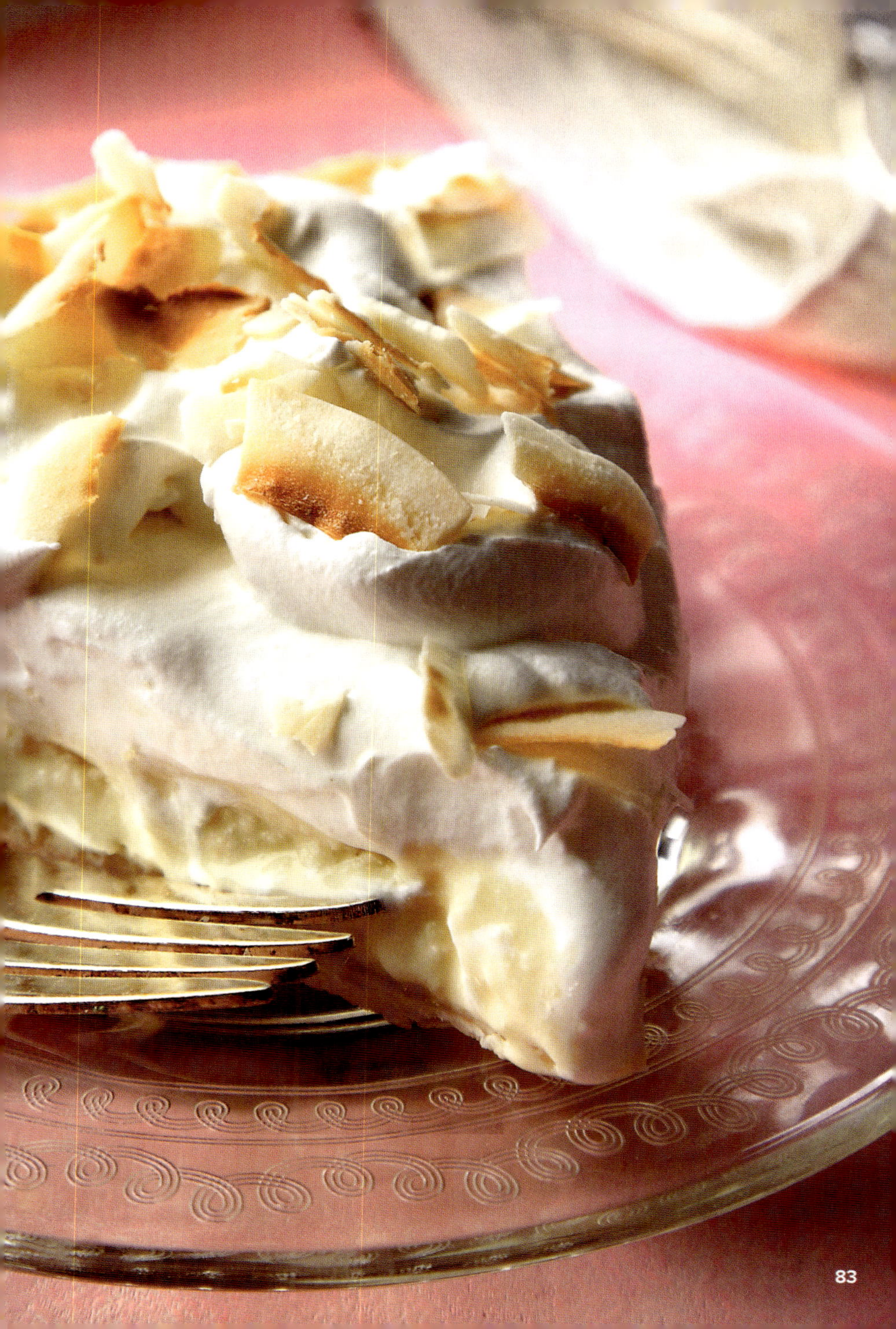

SWEET RECIPES

Buttermilk Pound Cake
with Vanilla Cream Cheese Frosting

Yield: 16 servings.

CAKE:
- 3 cups cake flour
- ½ teaspoon baking powder
- 3 sticks salted butter, softened
- 3 cups sugar
- 6 eggs at room temperature
- 1 cup buttermilk, warmed
- 1 teaspoon vanilla extract
- 1 teaspoon orange extract
- 1 teaspoon lemon extract

FROSTING:
- 6 ounces unsalted butter, softened
- 8 ounces cream cheese, softened
- 3 cups powdered sugar
- 2 tablespoons buttermilk
- 1 teaspoon vanilla extract

For the cake: Grease and flour a 9-inch tube cake pan. Mix together flour and baking powder; set aside. Cream together butter and sugar until light and fluffy. Add eggs, one at a time, mixing well. With the mixer on low speed, add the flour mixture a little at a time, alternating with buttermilk and ending with flour. Add extracts. Pour into prepared cake pan and place in cold oven. Bake at 350° for 1 hour and 15 minutes. Remove from oven, cover with aluminum foil, and let sit until cool.

For the frosting: In a large bowl, beat together the butter and cream cheese with an electric mixer. With the mixer on low speed, add the powdered sugar a cup at a time until smooth and creamy. Beat in the buttermilk and vanilla extract.

— Lynn Wells

Pineapple Pig Pickin' Cake

CAKE:
- 1 box butter golden cake mix
- 4 large eggs
- ¼ cup vegetable oil
- 1 (11-ounce) can mandarin oranges, chopped into smaller pieces, juice preserved

FROSTING:
- 1 (16-ounce) can crushed pineapple, drained
- 1 (3.4-ounce) box instant vanilla pudding
- 2 (8-ounce) containers whipped topping, thawed

For the cake: Preheat oven to 350°. Grease and flour 3 (8-inch) cake pans with vegetable shortening.

In a large bowl, combine cake mix, eggs, oil, and mandarin oranges with their juice.

Divide batter between pans. Bake 15 to 20 minutes, or until toothpick comes out clean.

Turn the cake out of the pan and place onto a wire rack. Let cool to room temperature.

For the frosting: In a large bowl, stir together the pineapple and pudding mix. Once combined, fold whipped topping into pineapple mixture.

Frost each layer and sides of the cake. Serve soon or loosely cover and refrigerate for up to 4 hours.

— *Mavis Brannon*

SWEET RECIPES

Cheerwine Poke Cake with Cream Cheese Glaze

Yield: 16 servings.

CAKE:

- 1½ cups Cheerwine (not diet), plus more for the cake mix (see below)
- 1 (3-ounce) box cherry gelatin
- 1 box white cake mix
- Ingredients for the cake mix, per package directions, substituting Cheerwine for water

GLAZE:

- 4 tablespoons unsalted butter, at room temperature
- 4 ounces cream cheese, at room temperature
- 1 teaspoon vanilla extract
- 2 cups powdered sugar
- 3 tablespoons milk
- ⅓ cup maraschino cherries, drained

For the cake: In a small saucepan, bring 1½ cups of Cheerwine to a boil. Remove from heat, add gelatin, and stir until dissolved. Pour into a bowl and refrigerate until needed.

Prepare the cake mix according to the package directions, substituting Cheerwine for the water. Bake in a 9 x 13-inch baking pan. Cool the cake in the pan on a wire rack for 15 minutes.

Use a chopstick, straw, or handle of a wooden spoon to poke holes in the cake in 2-inch intervals. Spoon the gelatin mixture evenly over the cake, letting it run down into the holes. Cover and refrigerate until chilled, at least 3 hours.

For the glaze: In a medium bowl, beat the butter, cream cheese, and vanilla until smooth. Add the powdered sugar in thirds, beating after each addition until smooth. Beat in the milk. Spoon the glaze over the top of the cake, spreading it to the edges. Sprinkle the cherries over the top.

— *Sheri Castle*

SWEET RECIPES

Honeydew Sorbet Float

Yield: 6 servings.

- 6 cups honeydew melon, cut into 1-inch chunks (approximately 2 melons)
- 2 tablespoons lemon juice
- 1½ cups cold water
- ¼ cup honey
- 1 bottle sparkling water or champagne, chilled

Fresh mint leaves (for garnish)

Place cut honeydew in a single layer on two parchment-lined baking sheets. Place baking sheets in the freezer for 4 hours or until melon is frozen.

Working in two batches, place half of the frozen melon in a high-powered blender or food processor, and add half quantities of the lemon juice, water, and honey. Blend until smooth. Repeat.

Pour melon mixture into a rectangular aluminum baking dish and cover surface of mixture with plastic wrap.

Place dish in the freezer for another 30 to 45 minutes until it sets.

To assemble the float, place 2 scoops of honeydew sorbet in 6 chilled glasses and top each with champagne or sparkling water. Garnish each serving with a fresh mint leaf.

— *Lynn Wells*

Banana Pudding

Yield: 12 servings.

PUDDING:
- 1 cup sugar
- ½ cup all-purpose flour
- ½ teaspoon salt
- 4 cups whole milk
- 4 large egg yolks, at room temperature
- 1 tablespoon butter
- 2 teaspoons pure vanilla extract
- 6 small ripe, firm bananas, cut into thin rounds (about 6 cups)
- 8 ounces vanilla wafers (about 60 cookies)

MERINGUE:
- 4 large egg whites, at room temperature
- ½ teaspoon cream of tartar
- ½ cup sugar

For the pudding: Whisk together the sugar, flour, and salt in a large, heavy saucepan or in the top of a double boiler. (If using a double boiler or a metal bowl sitting securely over a saucepan, fill the bottom pot about ⅓ full of water and bring to a simmer. The top pot should not touch the hot water.)

Add the milk in a slow, steady stream, whisking continuously until smooth. Whisk in the egg yolks. Cook over medium heat, stirring continuously with a heatproof spatula, until the pudding thickens and just begins to bubble around the edges, about 10 minutes. Remove the pan from the heat and stir in the butter and vanilla.

Line the bottom of a large, oven-safe serving bowl with vanilla wafers. Top with a layer of banana slices. Pour a thin layer of pudding over the bananas, spreading it with the spatula. Repeat the layers until you have used all of the remaining ingredients, ending with a top layer of pudding.

For the meringue: Preheat oven to 325°. Place the egg whites and cream of tartar in a clean, dry, spotless metal or glass bowl. Beat with an electric mixer set to medium speed until foamy. Increase the mixer speed to high and add the sugar in a slow, steady stream, beating until the meringue is glossy and stiff peaks form, 2 to 4 minutes. Spoon the meringue over the warm pudding, spreading to the edges of the bowl. Use the back of the spoon to make pretty swirls and peaks in the meringue.

Bake until the meringue is golden brown with toasted peaks, 15 to 20 minutes. Cool on a wire rack for 30 minutes. Serve slightly warm, or cool completely and refrigerate until chilled. — *Sheri Castle*

SWEET RECIPES

Blackberry Cobbler

Yield: 6-8 servings.

- 1 tablespoon + 6 tablespoons salted butter
- 1 large egg
- 1¼ cups all-purpose flour
- 1¼ cups + 2 tablespoons sugar
- 4 cups frozen or fresh blackberries
- 1 tablespoon fresh lemon juice
- Vanilla ice cream or whipped cream (optional)

Preheat oven to 375°.

Grease an 8 x 8-inch pan with 1 tablespoon of butter. In a separate bowl, combine the egg, flour, and 1¼ cups of sugar until the mixture resembles a coarse meal. Add ¼ cup of the flour mixture to the bottom of the pan. Pour in the blackberries and sprinkle the lemon juice on top. Spread the remaining flour mixture evenly over the blackberries. Melt 6 tablespoons of butter and pour on top. Sprinkle 2 tablespoons of sugar on top.

Bake for 40 minutes, or until crust is golden brown. Let sit for 10 minutes before serving.

Serve in individual ramekins and top with vanilla ice cream or whipped cream (optional). — *Lynn Wells*

SWEET RECIPES

Crook's Corner's Atlantic Beach Pie

Yield: 1 pie.

- 1½ sleeves of saltine crackers
- ⅓ to ½ cup softened unsalted butter
- 3 tablespoons sugar
- 1 can (14 oz) sweetened condensed milk
- 4 egg yolks
- ½ cup lemon or lime juice, or a mix of the two
- Fresh whipped cream and coarse sea salt for garnish

Preheat oven to 350°. Crush the crackers finely, but not to dust. You can use a food processor or your hands. Add the sugar, then knead in the butter until the crumbs hold together like dough. Press into an 8-inch pie pan. Chill for 15 minutes, then bake for 18 minutes or until the crust colors a little.

While the crust is cooling (it doesn't need to be cold), beat the egg yolks into the milk, then beat in the citrus juice. It is important to completely combine these ingredients. Pour into the shell and bake for 16 minutes until the filling has set. The pie needs to be completely cold to be sliced.

Serve with fresh whipped cream and a sprinkling of sea salt. — *Bill Smith*

Molasses Cream Pie Cookies

Yield: 2 dozen cookies or 1 dozen pies.

COOKIES:
- 1½ cups unsalted butter, softened
- 1 cup white granulated sugar
- 1 cup light brown sugar
- 2 large eggs
- ½ cup molasses
- 4½ cups all-purpose flour
- 2 teaspoons baking soda
- 3 teaspoons ground ginger
- 1 teaspoon ground cardamom
- 1½ teaspoons ground cinnamon
- 1 teaspoon ground cloves
- ¼ teaspoon salt
- ¾ cup coarse sugar or sparkling sugar

CREAM FILLING:
- 2 (7-ounce) jars marshmallow fluff
- ⅔ cup of shortening
- 4 cups confectioners' sugar
- 3 tablespoons warm water

For the cookies: Preheat oven to 350°. Using a mixer, cream together butter, white granulated sugar, and brown sugar until light and fluffy. Beat in eggs and molasses.

In a separate bowl, combine the flour, baking soda, ginger, cardamom, cinnamon, cloves, and salt; gradually add to butter mixture and mix well.

Shape into 2-inch balls and roll in coarse sugar. Place 2½ inches apart on parchment-lined baking sheets. Bake 13 to 15 minutes or until tops are cracked. Remove from oven and place cookies on wire racks to cool. Enjoy as is, or continue on to make cookie sandwiches.

For the cream filling: Using a hand mixer, mix together marshmallow fluff, shortening, and confectioners' sugar. Add warm water and mix well. Spread 1 to 2 tablespoons of filling on the bottom of each cookie and top with a second cookie. — *Lynn Wells*

SWEET RECIPES

Pecan Bourbon Pie

Yield: 8 servings.

- 1 unbaked refrigerated pie crust
- 4 eggs, lightly beaten
- 1 cup granulated sugar
- ½ cup light corn syrup
- ½ cup dark corn syrup
- ⅓ cup unsalted butter, melted
- 4 tablespoons bourbon
- 1 teaspoon vanilla extract
- 1 teaspoon salt
- 1 cup coarsely chopped pecans
- ½ cup pecan halves

Preheat oven to 375°. Place pie crust in pie pan and crimp the edges to form a decorative edge. Mix together eggs, sugar, corn syrups, butter, bourbon, vanilla, and salt until well blended.

Prick the sides and bottom of the pie shell with a fork. Spread the chopped pecans on the bottom and pour the egg mixture over them. Place pecan halves on top of egg mixture, forming a circle inside the edge of the pie crust.

Bake for 35 to 45 minutes, until just set around the edges but still slightly loose in the center. Place on a rack to cool slightly.
— *Lynn Wells*